Making
Customers
Matter

The Lessons Learned Series

Learn how the most accomplished leaders from around the globe have tackled their toughest challenges in the Harvard Business Press *Lessons Learned* series.

Concise and engaging, each volume in this series offers fourteen insightful essays by top leaders in industry, the public sector, and academia on the most pressing issues they've faced. The *Lessons Learned* series also offers all of the lessons in their original video format, free bonus videos, and other exclusive features on the 50 Lessons companion Web site: **www.50lessons.com/customers**.

Both in print and online, *Lessons Learned* contributors share surprisingly personal and insightful anecdotes and offer authoritative and practical advice drawn from their years of hard-won experience.

A crucial resource for today's busy executive, *Lessons Learned* gives you instant access to the wisdom and expertise of the world's most talented leaders.

Other books in the series:

Making Customers Matter

LES50NS

www.50lessons.com/customers

Boston, Massachusetts

Copyright 2010 Fifty Lessons Limited
All rights reserved

Printed in the United States of America
14 13 12 11 10   5 4 3 2 1

Library of Congress Cataloging-in-Publication Data
forthcoming

In partnership with 50 Lessons, a leading
provider of digital media content, Harvard
Business Press is pleased to offer *Lessons
Learned*, a book series that showcases the
trusted voices of the world's most experi-
enced leaders. Through the power of personal storytelling, each book in this series
presents the accumulated wisdom of some
of the world's best-known experts and offers
insights into how these individuals think,
approach new challenges, and use hard-won
lessons from experience to shape their leadership philosophies. Organized thematically
according to the topics at the top of man-
agers' agendas—leadership, change management, entrepreneurship, innovation, and
strategy, to name a few—each book draws
from 50 Lessons' extensive video library of
interviews with CEOs and other thought
leaders. Here, the world's leading senior

A Note from the Publisher

executives, academics, and business thinkers speak directly and candidly about their triumphs and defeats. Taken together, these powerful stories offer the advice you'll need to take on tomorrow's challenges.

As you read this book, we encourage you to visit **www.50lessons.com/customers** to view videos of these lessons as well as additional bonus material on this topic. You'll find not only new ways of looking at the world, but also the tried-and-true advice you need to illuminate the path forward.

☙ CONTENTS ☙

Contents

Making Customers Matter

Setting the Tone for Customer Advocacy

Jeb Dasteel

*Senior Vice President and
Chief Customer Officer, Oracle*

ONE OF THE great lessons learned for me in the role that I've been in at Oracle now for several years is that I can't be the only customer advocate; that, in fact, the tone has to be set from the top: from our board of directors, from our chairman, from our CEO, our presidents, and through the entire organization. Literally every single customer-facing employee has to, in some manner or another, be a customer advocate.

Every issue that's raised is addressed. Whether it's a big issue with a big customer, a big issue with a small customer, or a small issue with a small customer, those issues are addressed with equal intensity. Now, it's not that we respond in like manner for every situation, whether it's a very complex issue or not, but the issue is addressed. It goes through a triage process, no matter who the customer is and what the potential ramifications are, either to Oracle or to that customer.

One example that comes to mind is when Charles Phillips, our president, received a phone call from a customer in the United Kingdom. It happened to be a CIO of a relatively small customer of ours, who had some pretty serious issues that he needed to have resolved before he could go live with an Oracle call center solution. That solution was scheduled to go live on that Monday morning. He had maybe thirty-six hours to solve this problem. Our security office took the call because it was a Saturday. The call was immediately patched through to our president, who was in New York at the time. He called me within about a half an hour. Within, at most, an hour of that time, we had engineers, support personnel, and the account team in the United Kingdom—which is where the issue arose—all over this issue. By Monday morning, the problem was resolved.

That's an example that's like hundreds, if not thousands, of examples that crop up over the course of the year. It turned out in this particular case that the issue had absolutely nothing to do with Oracle software and had nothing to do with the Oracle services that were provisioned to support this customer. The point was that they were in a crisis, and the point was that they were having a pretty significant potential business impact. We were best positioned to solve the issue.

The lesson learned is setting the tone at the executive level. Every single Oracle executive, even our board of directors, has a high level of engagement with customers. It's expected. It's just a natural part of the role, whether you're the chairman, the CEO, or the president. All the way down through the entire organization, everybody has a customer-facing role. In fact, it's hard to find an employee anywhere in Oracle where there is not a customer-facing aspect to their role.

We literally have our board members sit in on advisory board meetings, where they can directly hear customers talking about their experiences with Oracle. Sometimes it's a great experience; sometimes it's not a great experience. But our board members and every management level in between the board and, say, the engineers in the development organization, hear this feedback. They understand what the feedback is. They can begin to see how Oracle responds to this sort of feedback. The lesson is all about setting the proper tone. That tone then becomes pervasive through the organization.

TAKEAWAYS

⚔ The tone for customer advocacy must be set by senior management, from the CEO and the board of directors down through to the rest of the organization.

⚔ The best customer service addresses all customer issues, without regard to the size of the customer or the size of the issue.

⚔ When board members sit in on meetings with customers, they can hear for themselves what the issues are, what feedback there is for the organization, and what the organization is doing to address the issues.

Personalize the Customer's Perspective

Barbara D. Stinnett

President, SumTotal Systems, Inc.

BEING A CHIEF customer officer, it's all about the customer. The first experience I had was my greatest. It was customer initiated.

When I started at Hewlett-Packard, I was right out of school; it was my first job, my first quota, the first sales calls and customers. On top of that, they had ten-thousand-plus products. We were over-whelmed with and focused upon creating what we had to offer the customer. It was all about what we were bringing to the client. To me, everything looked like a nail, and I had a hammer. I had several customers who would buy small pieces, but not many.

There was a gentleman who worked for Cray Research. He was their CIO at the time, Paul Schoenholtz. He was a tremendous gentleman for the job, just in his own right. He'd probably seen thousands of salespeople coming in, but he actually took an interest in me personally. One after-noon he said, "Let me buy you a pizza and a beer. Let's sit down and let me share a lit-tle bit about my life, so you get to know me better, and what it is to be a CIO."

He was a pretty smart guy. What he was doing was teaching me how to be customer-centric. Because—like most people that are actually in companies working with clients—sometimes you're nervous. You're focused on your own issues and what your goals are, such as, "I have to get this implemented at this account." You don't ever stop to think about what it is that the customer needs.

Early on—I was twenty-one at the time—over that pizza and beer, I learned a best practice that I had never thought of and probably wouldn't have if Paul Schoenholtz had not stopped to say, "You really need to understand who I am. Here's who I am. Here's what I care about. This is how I'm measured in my company. This is what happens if I make a bad selection." He made it personal. It caused a pause for me. I stopped and thought about what it was that I had to do. I needed to listen first. Then I needed to align, to be sure that what Hewlett-Packard had to offer was what Paul and Cray Research needed. We had to define where there were gaps. I learned about partnerships and realized that Hewlett-Packard couldn't be everything. We had to build an ecosystem and have things around that to solve the business problem. And then, lastly, I needed to execute.

It's something that sounds so simple; where you listen, you align, you define, and you execute. On paper it sounds basic, but it has much deeper meaning for me. It became the best practice for me as we moved forward.

The lesson that I learned from it was to take time to understand your audience. Understand the customer and what makes them tick. What are they being held accountable for? Then go back in and architect for the company that you work for. Do you have something that can help them solve their issues? Chances are, you do to some extent, whether it's 50 percent or 70 percent. Second, know who your partners are. Who else can you bring in to help solve that problem? When you sit down, treat that person—the customer—as if it's your own job with your own metrics. Figure out how to solve that problem together. That's what the listen, align, define, and execute is all about.

TAKEAWAYS

- Many people who work with clients are so focused on their goals and what they have to offer that they don't stop to think about what their customer needs.

- Make your customer relationship personal: when you sit down together, treat that customer's job and metrics as if they were your own.

- You need to listen to your customer to understand who he is, what he cares about, how he is measured, and what happens if he makes a bad selection.

- You need to align yourself and your organization with what you know about the customer in order to determine whether and how you can satisfy his needs.

Communicate Your Initial and Ongoing Value

Dave Mabon

Chief Customer Officer
GENCO Supply Chain Solutions

THE CHALLENGE WE all have is, "How do we drive customer behavior that is profitable for our company, as well as drive value for our customer?" It's an interesting challenge. Where the two come together is value.

Making Customers Matter

In our world as a service provider, many of our competitors will engage in an initiative for a client and provide value on an initial basis. They'll improve performance, reduce cost, and then they'll go about their business as usual until the contract comes up for renewal. An initiative that's worked well for us is the concept of initial and ongoing value. This is where we tie key performance indicators and performance expectations of our team to improving upon that customer's service offering, each and every year that we have the client. If we have a client for six years, you'll be able to see in year one the value we were able to deliver; then each subsequent year, what initiatives we put in place to reduce costs, improve performance, and improve our customer's customer satisfaction.

We also tie these initiatives to the compensation of our operations team. To the extent that we can achieve the projected productivity goals or exceed them, our operations team receives up to a 30 percent bonus on their salary for meeting and exceeding those initial and ongoing value goals.

One of the first customers that we applied this to was a popular apparel manufacturer. The contract was coming up for renewal; it was four years in the running. Of course their purchasing department comes in, and they don't care about the customer relationships or anything—they're the purchasing department. They started off down the typical path of, "You need to reduce your cost by this much; you need to do a, b, c, and d, or we'll put the business out to bid." We had prepared the initial and ongoing value data, and qualified—going back over the last four years of the contract—how we had saved money, improved performance, put most of their team through Six Sigma and Lean training, and increased or improved their cash-to-cash measurements. At the end of this presentation, where we showed them all the quantifiable results that we had delivered, they stopped and said, "You know what? We didn't realize, over the course of four years, how much value you've actually provided." We also gave them two or three angles that they might want to pursue next, in terms of future value.

The customer, in the end, didn't put the business out to bid. They reengaged with us for another four years. I think now we're happy we were able to provide more services. The customer's happy; they realize the value that was delivered. Now they've engaged in two of the four initiatives that we presented, and they're realizing the benefits of those today.

The lesson learned is, everyone provides value, and many of us provide value every day. But if you don't communicate the value you provide, it's like you didn't provide it at all.

TAKEAWAYS

- ❧ The concept of initial and ongoing value refers to improving upon the service offering to your customers each and every year.

- ❧ To ensure the best service and to motivate your teams, tie service improvement initiatives to the compensation of operations-team members.

- ❧ Everyone provides value—many of us provide value every day—but if you don't communicate the value you provide, it's like you didn't provide it at all.

The Tale of Two Service Initiatives

Tammy McLeod

Vice President and Chief Customer Officer, Arizona Public Service Company

A LESSON THAT I've learned about driving profitable customer behavior is what I'll call the tale of two service initiatives.

We measure many things, but a key interaction for us is when a customer connects to service. They call in; they connect service. That's our first opportunity to establish a reputation with them. Obviously, whatever opinion that they have at the end of that transaction is what they go away with around our company.

I had an idea to follow up with those customers. Let's go thirty, forty-five, sixty days out, after they've connected service, follow up with them, and ask, "How'd it go? We're just checking in with you. You should have received your first bill by now. Is there anything you don't understand? Do you have any questions about service? Can we check and make sure you're on the right rate for you?" Any of those types of follow-up questions.

We implemented something like that on a pilot basis. We selected a group of customers freshly connected, and we went after them forty-five to sixty days later. We did it with outbound dialer, and called them and followed up with them. In fact, we saw that we were moving the barometer on customer satisfaction, moving it forward. It was a good thing.

Two Service Initiatives

I'll contrast that to an idea that our marketing folks brought to me a few years back, which was not for new customers, but for existing customers. "Let's go out and work with air conditioning servicers in the area to buy down or create a good deal for people to have their air conditioning units serviced at the start of summer. We'll go out, we'll set up, and we'll work with one of the trade associations to set up this list of qualified contractors that our customers can go to for a reduced, well-priced tune-up." As you can imagine, AC units in Arizona in the summertime are a big deal. We went out, we set that up, and we did a little bit of cooperative advertising. As I said in the previous story, we moved the barometer forward.

What's interesting, though, is on those two stories, the important thing there was measuring it, and where we started from, and where we ended up.

When we're connecting new service, people are excited. They're moving into a new house; they're probably happy about whatever life-changing transformation has taken them to that situation. We were starting with a satisfied group. I was moving them up a couple of percentage points, obviously making them more satisfied. But in terms of the effort that we were putting into that, the follow-up and everything that was involved, it was probably not worth it. It had probably gotten to a point where I was actually over serving.

On the flip side, when we started with someone who'd been a customer maybe five, ten, fifteen years, and went out with a new product offering that not only benefited them with an AC tune-up, but showed them a long-term benefit to having a well-maintained unit that then reduced their electric bill, the needle moved much farther ahead. We were able to see, starting from a not-quite-as-satisfied group—because that new connect had worn off—we were able to move that needle ahead and take a group that was satisfied and push them into that very-satisfied group.

There are actually a couple of lessons that you learn from that. One is to measure everything. In comparing those two service offerings, knowing where we were starting, knowing where we ended up, allowed us to make a decision about where we made a bigger impact. We were able to be strategic with the service dollars.

The other big lesson for me was that it wasn't the idea that I liked the most. Again, the marketing idea that I came in with, I thought would be great. That wasn't the one where we got our biggest impact. Just because I like it does not necessarily make it a great idea. I have to remember constantly that I'm not the customer.

TAKEAWAYS

⊰ In order to improve their satisfaction levels, you may need to offer existing customers very different services from those that you offer new customers.

Making Customers Matter

⊰ It's important to measure everything;
you have to know where you're starting
and where you're ending up to understand where your service dollars are
having the greatest impact.

⊰ To provide the most impactful service
and value, you have to appreciate the
customer's perspective, which may be
very different from your own.

— ⊷ —

In Fast Moving Markets, Stay Close to Your Customer

— ⊷ —

Rudy Vidal

*Former Executive Vice President and
Chief Customer Officer, inContact, Inc.*

THE MOST IMPORTANT thing about setting customer strategy in a fast-paced market is that we tend to get caught up in our view. The market tends to shift faster than our view. The faster the market, the more we need to listen to the customer. It's about the voice of the customer. It's not what I think the customer wants. It's about what the customer actually needs.

When I was at Panasonic, we had large retail chains that were having difficulty selling one product. Their request to us was, "You need to lower the price because this product is not selling." The product was the leading product in the industry. Certainly it did not need a lowering of price, but the retailer thought that the price point was a bit too high. That's the reason why they couldn't sell it.

There was a faction in Panasonic that said, "We need to lower the price, because obviously, if we don't lower the price, they're going to drop the product." Somebody else said something interesting. He said, "You know what? It's been a month since I've visited that dealer." A month—imagine! That's not a long time, but—"It's been a month. I'm going to go out to that dealer again. Let's talk tomorrow."

He went out to the dealerships and spent a whole day at five different locations. He came back and said, "They don't need a lower price. They need demonstrators."

So we went back to the customer and said, "We would like to try something. At our cost, we would like to put demonstrators on your retail floor that will demonstrate the product so your customers will see the full value." They doubled their sales for that product.

They didn't need a lower price; they wanted a lower price. What they needed was value that they didn't know they had a need for, which was for people to understand the feature base of the product.

It's clear to me that when you have a fast-moving market, the customer strategy needs to start at the customer, not at our viewpoint of what we think the customer needs. What we think the customer needs is usually tainted by what we can provide or what we're ready to do. It's not usually inclusive of some out-of-the-box thing. This was an out-of-the-box idea. A sales guy at a lower level said, "What these guys need are demonstrators." It saved the product.

TAKEAWAYS

⧓ Markets change at a faster pace than our view of them changes.

⧓ The faster a market changes, the more important it is to listen to the voice of the customer in order to keep up.

⧓ In fast-moving markets, strategy needs to start with what the customer needs, not what we think the customer wants.

⧓ Our viewpoint of what the customer needs is usually tainted by what we can provide or what we're ready to do for her.

Engage Your Customers to Grow Your Business

Dan Wittner

Chief Customer Officer, RBM Technologies

ONE OF MY favorite stories about how we began the transformation of RBM Technologies to a more customer-centric organization, as opposed to a technologist organization, was actually my first meeting with RBM. They had brought me in as a consultant to help them improve the engagement with customers and prospects. They asked me to come and sit in on a WebEx-hosted demonstration with a telecommunications prospect.

I sat there for sixty-five minutes and listened to the team—the technologists at RBM—go through every aspect of the product without asking a single question of the prospect.

Sixty minutes later, after the engagement, the team—the technologists at RBM—asked, "Do you have any questions?" There were none. It was silent.

That was the last time the prospect was ever heard from, although the RBM team felt that the call had gone amazingly well, as they had gotten through every aspect of the product.

To me, that highlighted where the mindset of the RBM team was. They were a team of technologists as opposed to solutionists understanding what that prospect or even their clients had as needs, and talking to those needs, as opposed to talking about the product. So, it became Selling 101 right off the bat with RBM: to engage a prospect and a customer, to find out with probing questions, core questions, and a defined methodology what the objectives and needs were, and how we could address them immediately.

The transformation to customer-centricity basically changed the prospecting and sales engagement methodology by driving to make the customers talk to us, driving to have that prospect open up so we could learn and gain knowledge about what they were really looking to buy.

Engaging around the customers' most pressing need that correlates to your platform, showing them how that platform will drive value immediately from a key performance indicator, return on investment, or whatever type of measurement tool they're looking to utilize, and delivering upon that, is what you need to understand right away.

TAKEAWAYS

- ⚔ Customer-centric teams first learn and understand the needs of their prospects and clients and then speak to those needs, rather than speaking about their products.

- ⚔ When engaging a prospect or customer, use probing questions, core questions, and a defined methodology to determine their objectives and needs and how you can address them immediately.

- ⚔ Engage with your customer around the most pressing need that correlates to your platform and then demonstrate how your platform will drive value using whatever measurement the customer will utilize.

———■◆■———

Satisfying Customers

———■◆■———

Sir John Egan

Former Chief Executive, BAA

I'VE ALWAYS THOUGHT that the fundamental purpose behind a business is to make profits out of satisfying customers. If you explain what you're trying to do to your workforce, I think that's a wonderful starting point.

When I went to Jaguar Cars it was in a very powerless state; it was losing 30 percent

of net sales, and you really have to try hard
to lose that much money. I was trying to get
something that would bring the whole company together. I explained that the whole
purpose was to create cars of such quality
that the customers would be happy and satisfied with them.

Everybody in the company knew the processes we had in place to ask our customers
whether they were happy or not with the
car's performance and quality. We put in
place an absolutely indisputable measure
of quality. Then we implemented processes
to improve the quality. But once we'd done
that and made it easy to make the cars because the quality was good, productivity
almost automatically followed behind.

I went to BAA after running Jaguar
Cars, and I was quite clear that satisfying
customers was an absolutely core thing to
do. While you're learning a new business,
you wonder which of your tricks from the
past you should carry with you. Satisfying
customers was clearly one that was core to
my philosophy.

Satisfying Customers

I started a customer satisfaction index,
where we were constantly talking to passen-
gers about every process they went through,
to see what they were and weren't happy
with. This then informed management
about what they were doing well and badly.
The strategies for running the company
really came out of this kind of information.
Interestingly, one of the things that we were
doing worst of all was shopping.

People saw the airport as a rip-off; every
summer, newspapers went to our airports
and bought things very expensively, so the
"rip-offs" at the airport made huge head-
lines. It was the worst and least satisfactory
of the things that we did. We put together
a retailing program to satisfy the customer,
which turned out to be immensely profitable. You're probably now familiar with
all the shopping malls that you see not only
at BAA airports, but at airports all over
the world. It all started from satisfying the
customer.

I think a simple view of what you're trying
to do in your business—to make profit out

of satisfying customers—is a message that can be understood by your workforce; they can join in helping you to run the company. They know precisely what you're trying to do. Then your staff can help you in that fundamental mission: they understand what they're doing, and they understand why they're there. But once you get the quality right, you can then start to tackle productivity and improve that as well.

TAKEAWAYS

- The fundamental purpose behind a business is to make profits out of satisfying customers.

- The knowledge of what you're doing well and what you're doing badly from your customer's point of view can be used to drive company strategy.

Satisfying Customers

If you present your workforce with a simple view of what your business is trying to achieve, they will understand and join in helping you run the company.

Always Ask the Consumer

Lord Karan Bilimoria

Founder and CEO, Cobra Beer

AT EVERY STAGE of growing a business, whether it's right in the beginning when you've got your idea, or whether it's making major decisions along the way; always, always, always ask the consumer before you go forward. As an entrepreneur you've got to come up with the ideas, and never take those ideas forward without checking with the consumer.

Making Customers Matter

One of our earlier mistakes was when I went out to Bangalore, India, to set up the whole brewing project. My partner with whom I had started my business, Arjun Reddy, stayed back in England, and I went to Bangalore and spent three months there. My focus was to develop this beer that had never existed before, so we chose a brand that I went out to India with—I actually carried the artwork for the labels with me. We had chosen a brand called Panther—as in leopard—and I can still visualize this label; it was a very modern, cool label of the eye of a black panther. I very proudly handed this label to the printers and then focused on getting the product right and actually getting the beer and the other elements such as packaging right.

We were quite far down the road, and the first brew was actually about a week away from being bottled and shipped out to the United Kingdom when I got a frantic phone call from my partner in England, who said, "Karan, we've got a problem."

Always Ask the Consumer

I said, "What's happened?"

He replied, "Well, we've been trying out Panther with the trade and with consumers, and nobody likes it."

I had a choice there. We were running up against time, and I could have said, "Well, forget it, we've chosen Panther, we're going to run with Panther. Who cares what anyone said?"

I told him, "Well, no, actually, let's just stop. What was the next name on the list?"

Of course, we'd gone through hundreds of names, and the next name was Cobra. I said, "Try out Cobra, and I'll stop the presses."

I went to the printers, but by then they'd already started. They said it was too late. I said, "Look, you have to stop, you've got to wait. Give me a few days."

I got a phone call from my partner after two days, and he explained they had been trying out Cobra and that everybody loved it.

I said, "Great! Well, back to the drawing board." So we literally had to design the Cobra beer label from scratch. Everything got delayed and we lost some money, but I'm so glad that I made that decision.

The lesson learned was that, as an entrepreneur, you've got to come up with the ideas but never, ever go forward with them before you've checked them out with the consumers.

In the early days of developing business, a lot is about survival and you can't afford focus groups and intensive and expensive research, but what you can always do is informal research. You can always get feedback from consumers in lots of different ways that cost no money whatsoever, and even now, when we're a much larger company, we do carry out focus groups and intensive research. We will always carry out our informal research as well because I really value it, and there are lots of opportunities when you can do this.

So, for example, in the early days we would exhibit at trade shows and consumer shows at every opportunity to get our brand in front of consumers. At every one of these shows we would always conduct a survey with the consumers to get feedback on the product. We were always looking for feedback from consumers about the taste, the packaging, and marketing ideas.

Once, I remember, we had a big challenge in our business; in 1996 our sales doubled in a calendar year, and our problems of importing Cobra beer from India quadrupled. We then had to make a very tough decision. We'd built up this brand as an imported Indian beer—the biggest-ever export beer out of India—and we then had to think of actually producing it here in the United Kingdom.

I was terrified of doing that. I thought, "What will happen? Will my consumers stop drinking the product because it's now brewed over here in the United Kingdom?" Although 85 percent of the well-known lager brands are actually brewed under license in the United Kingdom, I was scared. And what do you do in that situation? You ask the consumer.

We were conducting our surveys as usual, and we slipped in a question to rank in order of importance the following four things about Cobra beer: the fact that it's an extra-smooth, less gassy lager; the fact that it's brewed to an authentic Indian recipe; the fact that it's a premium lager; the fact that it's imported from India.

The most important thing to the thousands of consumers surveyed in London and in the Midlands was the extra-smooth taste—by a long shot.

The least important thing to the consumer, by a long shot, was "imported from India."

Thumbs up, I'm brewing in the United Kingdom, and that's the reassurance you can get when you're close to your consumers; you can make major decisions. Always be really, really close to the consumer and get their feedback before moving on.

-------●••■-------

TAKEAWAYS

-------●••■-------

- ⚔ As an entrepreneur you've got to come up with the ideas, but never go forward with them before you've checked them out with consumers.

- ⚔ Short-term delays and losses may be preferable to the risks of ignoring market research that indicates consumers will not support your ideas.

- ⚔ In the early days of developing a business, when you can't afford focus groups and intensive and expensive research, you can always do informal research to stay close to your consumers.

Listen to the Changing Needs of the Consumer

Paul Skinner

CEO, Shell Oil Products Company LLC

WHATEVER BUSINESS you're in, whether it's retail, industrial, or another, you have to think consistently about customers and their changing needs, because that's how you achieve sustained marketing success and competitive advantage.

Making Customers Matter

One of the most powerful lessons that I had in my long career with Shell was in the context of the Shell retail business. It's a large business with more than fifty thousand outlets throughout the world and probably in excess of twenty million customers a day coming into the retail network. We saw considerable change in the way this business was managed during the 1990s. The traditional Shell approach to its retail business was to view our primary customer as the dealer—the operator of the retail side—as opposed to the many millions of individuals who were pumping gasoline or shopping in our shops.

As we changed our business structure toward being more globally managed throughout the 1990s, one of the things we did was to begin to resource that business with frontline retail professionals who'd come to us from the food business. We also had a team of product specialists from the fast-moving consumer goods industry who were very familiar with branded propositions. The arrival of these new people and the teams they set up really caused the business to focus much more on those end customers: the people who really matter.

We saw a tremendous shift in the level of understanding of the customer in that particular part of the Shell business. This was enormously helpful in framing the customer value propositions that we were putting forward. The introduction across the world of a range of differentiated premium fuels was particularly successful. This was based on deep consumer research and understanding. It enabled us to offer a premium range of fuels in most of our major markets based on a well-researched and well-executed customer value proposition. Without that much deeper understanding of the customer, I doubt we would have got there.

That's an example in terms of product development and innovation, but the general day-to-day management of our retail sites moved to a completely different plane as a result of having the business managed and driven by people for whom the retail business was their lifeblood. What we saw, over four or five years, was a tremendous shift in the attitude of the company toward this part of its business. It was reflected in positive progress in market share and profitability in most of our major markets. From this experience, I learned that a real understanding of customers, their needs, and their likely responses to new value propositions is absolutely essential in such a business.

TAKEAWAYS

- Whatever business you're in, you have to think consistently about customers and their changing needs in order to achieve sustained success and competitive advantage.

- Understanding your customer through deep consumer research is essential for framing the value proposition of your offerings.

- Shifting focus to the end consumers of your products and placing appropriately skilled and motivated professionals at the front lines of service can position you for improved market share and profitability.

———✦———

Service Beyond
the Call of Duty

———✦———

Gerry Roche

Senior Chairman, Heidrick & Struggles

I HAVE SEVERAL favorite service stories,
and we are a personal service business.
Frankly, I think everybody's in the service
business, including General Motors and
AT&T. We have products, but they are
dormant without service.

Ten years ago, we took Paul Anderson
out of Duke Energy into BHP in Australia,

the largest energy and mining company in the Pacific basin. We wound up getting Anderson almost signed up, practically saying yes, and we got him and his wife and their dog on an airplane going to Australia.

They land in Australia, and the customs people say, "No, no, you can't take that dog off that airplane on this land."

That night, Paul, instead of seeing the BHP people, had to get a boat, put the dog on the boat, anchor it six miles offshore and try to figure out what the hell to do with the dog. I got a wire from his wife, Maggie—quite a lady—which said, "Our dog can't get into Australia. If our dog can't get into Australia, I won't go to Australia. If I don't go to Australia, Paul's not going to Australia."

I could milk this story and make it longer, but I'll just say that we pulled strings in Washington and Australia to get the damn dog in, and I wrote a long letter telling Paul what he had to do. He had to go to this place and get this notarized, and it was all about getting the dog through customs and getting him into Australia. My final line was in longhand, where I wrote, "I hope this does the trick. Paul, is this what my job has come to?"

And he sends it back to me with one word on it. What do you think that word was?

"Yes."

Here I am, supposedly the world's head honcho headhunter, and I'm getting a dog into Australia. That's service! And I would say that if there's a lesson to be learned from the bottom line of service, it's to give people more than they expect, and don't ever, ever come close to the idea of saying, "Sorry, that's not my table."

Sam Walton, the founder of Walmart, Bentonville, Arkansas, before it got to be as big as it is today, got a blistering letter from an alleged customer. The letter said, "The tires we bought from your store wore out too quickly, and we are very disappointed with the quality of these tires and with Walmart. We've been shopping there for a long time, and this may well put our customer relationship with Walmart in jeopardy." Signed, Joe Blow.

Making Customers Matter

A day or two later, Joe Blow winds up getting four new beautiful Firestone tires with a nice letter from Sam saying, "Dear Whoever-you-are, hope you get under separate cover the tires that we've sent. We're sorry that you had so much trouble with them. We're sorry for your perception that this was caused by Walmart. Sam Walton. P.S. By the way, we don't sell tires."

That's a true story.

Going beyond what's expected, almost beyond the reasonable, is what service is all about. In this world which we're in, where it's much, much more about services as opposed to products, I think these lessons on service are absolutely fundamental.

As a last lesson: I was born and reared in a grocery store—what we refer to in this country as a mom-and-pop because there's a mom and pop behind the counter running the store. I was maybe seven or eight years old. I was behind the counter helping to serve Mrs. Davis. She was one of our best customers. For some reason I got snippy. I don't remember what I said, but I remember what happened.

Beyond the Call of Duty

My father grabbed me by the collar and dragged me into the kitchen, which was behind the store, and he said, "Gerry, let me make one thing clear to you. Mrs. Davis is one of our best customers. If she stops buying here, we can't afford for you to have dinner here. If we don't have customers, you don't eat. Do you understand that, Gerry?"

I never forgot that lesson. He made me go back into the store and apologize to Mrs. Davis and carry her bags home for her.

When people ask me where I learned to do this business, I say, "At a grocery store in Scranton, behind the counter when I was eight years old, thanks to Joe Roche, the grocer."

TAKEAWAYS

- ⚔ Give people more than they expect, and don't ever, ever come close to the idea of saying: "Sorry, that's not my table."

- ⚔ Going beyond what's expected, almost beyond the reasonable, is what service is all about.

- ⚔ Lessons in service are fundamental in a world where services are more important than products.

—◆◆◆—

Maintaining Customer Service When You Scale

—◆◆◆—

Richard T. Santulli

Former Chairman and CEO, NetJets, Inc.

BIG IN THIS BUSINESS is actually very important. Scale is important. The more airplanes you have—and we obviously have more than anybody else, no one comes anywhere close—it makes it easier to handle and take care of our customers. If an airplane breaks, the chances that we have one close by are a lot better than if we had two hundred airplanes. If an airplane breaks anywhere in the world, we know we can get there quicker than anyone else can.

Scale is very important. What we have to do is basically explain to our owners why that's important, why it's good for them. But then we can't make them feel that we're too big a company to care. The way we do that is very simple actually: customer service—we call it owner service. We set up teams, and we have only a certain number of customers per team.

Let's say there are seven people on a team and you have—I'm just making this up—one hundred fifty customers that will call that one team only. They will get to know the people that they're speaking to on the telephone. They'll always speak to one of those seven people and, more likely than not, they'll ask for one that they've been more familiar with.

Our team members get to know the customers very well; they know their likes, their dislikes. Even though we have that all on a computer, it's still very important when the person on the other end knows whether you are taking your dogs this time. And we'll make sure there are cookies on the plane for you. Or know whether your nanny is coming. Or if it's your anniversary, whether your wife likes Dom Pérignon or Cristal champagne. And we won't just read from a computer; we get to know the person so our owner still feels like it's a small company. When we started and we built it to one hundred owners, they felt like it was a small company. We had to maintain that. Now we have three thousand owners, and the way we do that is by having owner service teams that are specifically involved with and deal with a certain number of owners.

And then the events make them feel like it's a small company. We'll have the big events in New York City, Los Angeles, and Chicago. But then we'll have events in Phoenix and Dallas, in places all around the United States. We're doing an *American Idol*

event right now. We have meet-and-greets.
We have a deal with *American Idol*, where we
have tickets to thirty-five venues, but we also
have meet-and-greets with all the *American
Idol* people.

You may say, "Your customers like
American Idol?"

Absolutely. For their kids and grandkids
it's spectacular. And we'll do it in all the lit-
tle cities. We'll do it in Tampa and Fort
Lauderdale. The people, again, feel special;
and the brand to them becomes part of their
family. To them, that's not the feeling of a
big company; that's the feeling of a small
company. We do that and maintain that.
And that's very important because once
we're perceived as a big company, from
something other than operations, from a
customer service point of view, we lose. And
we just can't allow that to happen.

TAKEAWAYS

◄ For businesses where scale is essential
   to smooth operations and profitability, the way you maintain the feeling
   of a small company is by having service
   teams that are specifically involved
   with and deal with a limited number
   of customers.

◄ Service team members who know
   your customers and their preferences
   on a personal level create a feeling
   of intimacy characteristic of smaller
   organizations.

◄ Hosting special events wherever your
   customers are located makes customers
   feel special and enables your brand to
   become part of their family.

Using Customer Interactions to Improve Your Business

Maxine Clark

Chief Executive Bear
Build-A-Bear Workshop, Inc.

JUST ABOUT ANY interaction with your customer works; it's just how you use that information that really makes the difference.

Making Customers Matter

My happiest moments are when I walk into a mall and I spend time with our customers in the store. I walk in and nobody knows who I am. I can just be a customer. I can interact with the customers walking in our store and participate, and I can have a communication with them before they know that I'm the founder and chief executive bear. That's probably the best experience I could have.

Sometimes that doesn't last very long because the store person knows who I am. When the customers find out who I am, I get another side of the story. They'll say things like, "I have to tell you this story," "I have to tell you about one of the things I've always wanted," or, "My daughter has some ideas for you." They'll start to talk to me about ideas, and we will have that verbal experience.

We use the Internet for communicating back and forth in surveys with our customers. Our customers rate our guest experience every single week, and we've been doing that since the beginning, since our very first store opened in the St. Louis Galleria. We have a virtual cub advisory board, where we send products out to children via the Internet or directly through the mail for them to test and communicate about. We've developed our virtual world exactly that way, with children having experiences with us and with other virtual worlds. We incorporate those experiences.

I don't think anyone really expects you to do everything that they say. A lot of companies are afraid to ask questions of their customers, because if they don't do what the customers suggest, they'll think the company didn't listen. People don't think like that, especially children. They're very willing to give you what's in their hearts.

That's really what we're about; that's the essence of our brand. It's really about putting this love and feeling into this teddy bear. We figuratively put a heart and soul into it. If we don't live that, if we don't really feel that way about our customers and the whole experience, then I don't think we could create the kind of products that we do. We couldn't create that kind of connection with our customers.

It's actually the thing that I like to do the best. I feel cheated if I haven't had a customer connection every single day. I don't get them all one-on-one every day, but I do get them through e-mails and letters that we get from our customers. We share those publicly; in our company, it's part of our culture. The customer is always present. We can't bring them here, but they're here in spirit, and their letters are read to other people. They're shared across the company so people can see the good things that customers like and the things that they wish might be different.

For me and all the associates at Build-A-Bear Workshop, the essence of the customer experience is that it doesn't all rest with us. We don't have to have every idea; we don't have to have thought of every single detail. We listen to our customers, and they are very willing to share with us and help us. They're vested in our business. They grow our business through their ideas. If you look at that as the investment the customer is making in you, and you welcome that into your business, then you are going to grow.

That goes the same way for our associates in our stores. They know that we want to be better every single day. That's a core value in our company: bringing joy to people's lives every single day. We focus on growing and changing as the situation warrants it. How would we know if we weren't listening to our customers? They know best, and our store associates are right there on the front line with them. For us it's about a constant dialogue and communication.

We also work that backwards. We don't change things in our company without explaining to our associates why we're making that change. That way they understand. So many companies just put out an edict. They don't realize what kind of impact it's going to have on the customer experience in their store or their associate experience. To us, those things are not separate; they're the same.

TAKEAWAYS

- ﹅ Every interaction with your customers can be productive; it's how you use the information that makes the difference.

- ﹅ If you look at customer ideas and feedback as an investment the customer is making in you, and you welcome them into your business, then you are going to grow.

- ﹅ Sharing customer feedback internally, so people can see what customers like and what they wish might be different, keeps the customer present within your organization.

- ﹅ How associates are treated and communicated with has a direct impact on the customer experience; the two experiences are not separate.

———◆◆◆———

Customers Give You Feedback Every Day

William Lamar, Jr.

Former Chief Marketing Officer
McDonald's USA

———◆◆◆———

I'M GOING TO TELL a story about customer satisfaction and how it's used to really measure and also drive our sales. I'm going to talk about coffee as an example.

Making Customers Matter

Breakfast is one of our strengths, and we really are the dominant player in breakfast in our industry. Yet, while everything else at breakfast was growing and we were receiving very acceptable customer feedback and getting good measures of customer satisfaction overall, the major exception was our coffee. Coffee was a product area where we got complaints from customers consistently and where, when we did any kind of quantitative measures, we saw that our feedback on what customers felt about that coffee was relatively poor. We decided to tackle it.

As we dug into it, we found a couple of interesting things. The first is that no matter what product you sell you have to stay focused and have attention on the detail of that product. As people's tastes were becoming more sophisticated about coffee, their expectations of what they wanted from their coffee grew. We didn't grow with it. We didn't do the things with coffee that a good coffee requires. The second thing that we had done is that we had allowed ourselves to become kind of laissez-faire about coffee.

Feedback Every Day

We had more than fifty different blends
of coffee around the country. So we had
to step back and make some decisions about
that.

The customer feedback said, "If you want
me to buy your coffee, you have to make it
better."

Now the customers don't tell you how to
make it better, but they tell you that you have
to make it better. So we did. We basically
came down and worked on it and developed
two blends of coffee for the United States.
We implemented that program. We also
changed the imagery around our coffee
through what we did with our graphics, our
cups, and our lids, as we tried to make the
coffee more contemporary—as we've done
with the overall brand. We had great success.
The sales of coffee since we made those
changes have now grown more than fifty
percent. As important, it's given us credibil-
ity with consumers who are coffee drinkers
and is now allowing us to move into the
espresso-based coffees that are popular
with people today—lattes, cappuccinos,

etc.—which will be a great business opportunity for us.

The thing I learned, when I look back on what we did with coffee, is what a good marketer should never forget, but we always do, and that is, customers give you feedback every day. The most important feedback they give you is whether they buy what you're selling. Often we lose sight of the most basic. And I always remind myself: the customer knows what he or she wants in most instances. Your job is to figure out how to give it to them and make a profit on it.

TAKEAWAYS

- ⚔ No matter what product you sell, you have to stay focused and keep attention on the detail of that product.

- ⚔ Customers tell you that you have to make your product better but they don't tell you how.

- ⚔ The most important feedback customers give you is whether they buy what you're selling.

- ⚔ In most instances, the customer knows what he or she wants; your job is to figure out how to give it to them and make a profit on it.

Look to Your Consumers for Innovation

William Johnson

Chairman, President, and CEO
H. J. Heinz Company

INNOVATION IS THE differentiating aspect between successful long-term companies and those that die with a short lifespan. And I think the focus in innovation always has to be a couple of things. First, you have to be prepared to take risks, which means you have to be prepared to make mistakes. Second, innovation oftentimes depends on good judgment rather than good research.

The best example is plastic, squeezable ketchup, which we launched in 1982–1983 and which I was intimately involved with. We were moving from an iconic bottle that had been in the marketplace for close to a hundred years, going to a plastic squeeze bottle that was not ownable in terms of shape; it was a generic bottle available to us by a supplier at that time, American Can. We did a lot of research on the bottle, and most people in the company were predisposed not to change from the iconic glass bottle. But we did two things at that time that fundamentally shifted thinking.

First, we took our competitive product and put it in the squeeze bottle and tested it versus our iconic bottle—their brand, our brand—and concluded that consumers would switch from our brand to their brand because of the convenience of the package and the ability of the package to quickly dispense the product.

Second, the research came back and said, "Well, plastic ketchup, or really squeezable ketchup, is a good idea. It's going to hurt you if you don't do it, but it's only going to be 10 percent of the business."

Today it's 100 percent of the business.

So the research literally led us into thinking that certain elements of capacity were going to be saved and could be used again, and we only needed to add a little capacity on the plastic bottle. Upon launch in late 1982, early 1983, we ran out of capacity. Now one of the most unpleasant things in a marketer's life is going to the customer and telling him that we can't supply the product. The research led us to that conclusion.

I learned a number of lessons. One, is that if research was always right, nobody would ever make a mistake. Yet 95 percent of new products fail within six months of launch. Two, is that new products cannot, and research cannot, predict consumer behavior. What predicts consumer behavior is consumer behavior, which means you have to become intimate with your consumers. You have to be knowledgeable about them, understand them, and talk to them. You have to engage them in the process. They can never tell you what they want, but they can tell you what they are unhappy with, and then a clever marketer will figure out how to solve that problem.

The plastic squeeze bottle was very successful for twenty-five years or so, and then we were getting a number of complaints from consumers over the time, because the product evacuated so quickly that two things were happening. One is that there was a sort of film, crust, that covered the top of the package, and second, it was evacuating so fast that sometimes it created what is called serum separation, which is the water separating from the tomato solids. So we began to explore ways about how to solve this problem. We went into consumers' homes, and we discovered something, which, as my wife said later, "All you had to do was ask me, and I'd have told you this."

People were storing their ketchup upside down, and the reason they were storing their ketchup upside down was because when it evacuated from the bottle, they wouldn't get that serum separation and because they felt that this way nobody would see that crust forming at the top when it was standing up in the refrigerator. Therefore, we came up with the top-down bottle.

I'd love to say that it was a brilliant insight of inspiration, but basically it was what consumers were doing and we simply adopted and adapted it to what was available in the marketplace. The great breakthrough there was the silicon valve that allowed us to keep the evacuation in a simple stream and then prevent any crust from forming on the top of the package, which was a huge success.

There are any number of those kinds of stories, but innovation is fundamentally understanding your consumer, engaging them in the process, and listening to what concerns them and what they worry about and what they think about.

The second part is making sure that you engage not only your consumers but also your customers so that the product will know where to fit on the shelf. Customers may have a unique perspective on this. For example, we did not engage our food service customers right away, and so we launched the plastic package primarily through retail and then did the same with the upside-down package. We never took it to our food service customers. Then we found they were buying the plastic and upside-down packages at the grocery stores because their consumers were the same consumers going to the grocery stores and asking for the product. So it's the kind of thing where you need a full discussion not only with your consumers but also with your customers.

The third thing we learned is that the research is only directional. You have to use it as a guide, but you can't replace judgment. And that's where, again, I think an insight and an intellect and a curiosity about what's going on in the world are really sacrosanct in being successful from an innovation standpoint.

—◆—

TAKEAWAYS

—◆—

⚔ Some of the best innovations simply adopt and adapt what consumers are already doing in the marketplace.

⚔ The only indicator that predicts consumer behavior is consumer behavior, which means you have to become intimate with your consumers; you have to be knowledgeable about them, understand them, talk to them, and engage them in product and service development.

⚔ Innovation is, fundamentally, understanding your consumer, engaging

them in product development, and
listening to what concerns them, what
they worry about, and what they think
about.

⚔ Research is only directional; you can
use it as a guide, but it can't replace
judgment.

⧼ ABOUT THE ⧽ CONTRIBUTORS

Lord Karan Bilimoria is the Founder of Cobra Beer, a premier brewing company.

Lord Bilimoria started his career at Ernst & Young in 1982, where he spent four years working in audit, tax, training, and accounting. He qualified as a chartered accountant in 1986 and graduated in law from Cambridge University in 1988. He then worked at Cresvale in London (part of S&W Beresford) as a consulting accountant.

In 1989, he moved to *European Accounting Focus* magazine as its Sales and Marketing Director. Later that year, he founded Cobra Beer, realizing his ambition to develop a premium lager brewed to appeal to ale drinkers and lager drinkers alike.

Lord Bilimoria then extended into other markets with the launch of General Bilimoria Wines in 1999 and *Tandoori Magazine* and tandoorimagazine. com. He also founded curryzone.com, and is the Founder and Chairman of Cobrabyte Technologies.

In addition, Lord Bilimoria is Chairman of the Indo British Partnership, Chairman of the government's National Employment Panel's Small and Medium-Sized Enterprise Board, and Vice Chairman of the London Chamber of Commerce and Industry's Asian Business Association. He is a member of the Advisory Board of Boston Analytics.

Maxine Clark is the Chairman and Chief Executive Bear for Build-A-Bear Workshop, Inc., an inter-active, make-your-own stuffed animal retail-entertainment experience.

From November 1992 until January 1996, Ms. Clark was the President of Payless ShoeSource, a leading footwear retailer. Prior to joining Payless, Ms. Clark spent more than nineteen years in vari-ous divisions of the May Department Stores Com-pany, including merchandise development, merchandise planning, merchandise research, marketing, and product development.

In 1997 she founded Build-A-Bear Workshop and has served as its Chief Executive Bear from the beginning. She served as President from 1997 to 2004, and she became Chairman in April 2000.

Ms. Clark is a Director of the J. C. Penney Company, Inc. She also serves on the boards of the International Council of Shopping Centers and Washington University in St. Louis, and is a Director of BJC Healthcare, a nonprofit health-care organization.

Jeb Dasteel is Senior Vice President and Chief Customer Officer at Oracle, the world's leading supplier of software for information management and the second-largest independent software company.

About the Contributors

Early in his career, Mr. Dasteel held various management positions with defense contractors General Dynamics and Loral Corporation in materials, subcontracts, and program management. He then worked as an IT strategy and operations principal consultant at Gemini Consulting Group, a health care consultancy working in the United States, the United Kingdom, and Ireland.

Mr. Dasteel joined Oracle in 1998 and has served in various roles, including sales, consulting, and corporate management. In his current position, he focuses on driving profitable customer behavior and creating a customer-centric culture.

Mr. Dasteel graduated from San Diego State University and received his MBA from the University of San Diego and the Clairemont Graduate School. He was recently honored with the 2009 Chief Customer Officer of the Year Award by the Chief Customer Officer Council, a peer-led advisory networking group.

Sir John Egan is the former Chief Executive of BAA. Currently, he serves as Chancellor of Coventry University, a position to which he was appointed in March 2007.

From 1968 to 1990, Sir John developed a successful career in the automotive industry, working for General Motors and British Leyland. He joined British Leyland as Chairman of Jaguar Cars, rising to become Chairman and Chief Executive of Jaguar in May 1980. When Jaguar was privatized in August 1984 he remained as Chairman and Chief Executive.

After the takeover by Ford, Sir John retired from Jaguar and was appointed to the Board of Directors of BAA in June 1990, taking up the position of Chief Executive in September 1990, which he held until October 1999.

Sir John was also Chairman of the Construction Task Force. Its report, "Rethinking Construction," was commissioned by the Deputy Prime Minister, John Prescott, and was published in July 1998.

Sir John is a former Chairman of Inchcape (until 2006), Harrison Lovegrove, and Asite. He joined the Board of Severn Trent in October 2004 and became Chairman in January 2005.

William Johnson is the Chairman, President, and Chief Executive Officer of the H. J. Heinz Company, the most global of all U.S.-based food companies.

Mr. Johnson joined Heinz in 1982 as General Manager—New Businesses for Heinz USA. In 1984 he was promoted to Vice President—Marketing for Ketchup, Foodservice, and Sauces. He was named President and CEO of Heinz Pet Products in 1988, and assumed leadership of Star-Kist Foods, Inc., in May 1992, when the pet food business and Star-Kist Seafood, a sister Heinz affiliate, remerged.

In 1993 Mr. Johnson was named Senior Vice President of Heinz and joined the company's Board of Directors. His responsibilities included Heinz operations in the Asia/Pacific area, including Australia, New Zealand, China, Thailand, and South Korea, in addition to the canned tuna and pet food businesses of Star-Kist Foods, Inc. Mr. Johnson became President and Chief Operating Officer of Heinz in June 1996, and assumed the position of President and Chief Executive Officer in April 1998. He was named Chairman, President, and Chief Executive Officer in September 2000.

Prior to joining Heinz, Mr. Johnson was employed with Drackett, Ralston Purina, and Anderson-Clayton.

Mr. Johnson is a member of Emerson's Board of Directors, where he serves on the compensation committee. He is a Director of the Grocery Manufacturers of America and of UPS, and is an active member of the University of Texas McCombs School of Business Advisory Council.

William Lamar, Jr. is the former Chief Marketing Officer for McDonald's USA, a position he held from August 2002 until his retirement in 2008.

Mr. Lamar spent twenty-five years at McDonald's. For more than five years, he served as Vice President and General Manager of the Atlanta region, where he oversaw more than seven hundred restaurants. As Chief Marketing Officer, Mr. Lamar was responsible for national marketing, new product development, and business research for almost fourteen thousand U.S. restaurants. He is best known as the man behind the highly successful "I'm lovin' it" marketing campaign.

About the Contributors

In 2004 Mr. Lamar was honored as "Marketer of the Year" by *Advertising Age*, and in 2006 he was named one of the most powerful African-Americans in corporate America by *Black Enterprise* magazine.

In 2007 Mr. Lamar received the Chicago Advertising Federation's Silver Medal Lifetime Achievement Award for outstanding marketing leadership.

Dave Mabon is Chief Customer Officer for GENCO Supply Chain Solutions, North America's second-largest U.S-based third-party logistics provider.

In his role as CCO, Mr. Mabon is responsible for enhancing existing and new customer relationships across GENCO's diverse business units and developing strategies that grow the company. He came to GENCO with more than eighteen years of logistics sales and marketing experience.

From 1995 to 2007, Mr. Mabon worked for Kuehne + Nagel (formerly USCO Logistics), a global leader in worldwide contract logistics. Mr. Mabon was Senior Vice President of Sales and Marketing; directing sales, marketing, and business development for the Contract Logistics Unit. He participated in the sale of USCO to Kuehne + Nagel in 2001 and assisted in growing the company more than 300 percent through a series of senior sales and marketing roles.

From 1989 to 1995, Mr. Mabon was Director of Sales at the transportation services company American President Lines (APL).

About the Contributors

Mr. Mabon graduated from Northwestern University in 1989.

Tammy McLeod is Vice President and Chief Customer Officer for Arizona Public Service Company (APS). A subsidiary of Pinnacle West Capital, APS is the largest electric utility in Arizona, serving nearly a million customers.

Ms. McLeod began her career as a project manager for Whitbread and Company, the United Kingdom's largest hotel and restaurant company operating market-leading businesses in the budget hotels and restaurant sectors.

Ms. McLeod next worked with Jostens Learning Corporation (later renamed Compass Learning). She then worked in a variety of marketing and management roles in the software industry, including Educational Management Group. EMG, now part of Simon & Schuster, developed and distributed customized multimedia instructional materials and live interactive television services.

Ms. McLeod joined APS in 1995, serving as General Manager of Marketing, Customer Service and Southern Arizona Operations, before her promotion to Vice President and CCO. Her current responsibilities include management of statewide customer service operations, customer marketing, research, credit and collections, and call center. She also oversees Corporate Communications and Community Development.

About the Contributors

Ms. McLeod holds a Bachelor of Science from the University of Colorado and an MBA from the Wharton School at the University of Pennsylvania. She was recently appointed to the executive committee of the Greater Phoenix Economic Council.

Gerry Roche is the Senior Chairman of the executive search firm Heidrick & Struggles.

In his early career Mr. Roche was an account executive for the American Broadcasting Company; a sales manager, product manager, and marketing director for Mobil Oil Company's plastics subsidiary, Kordite Corporation; and a management trainee at AT&T.

Following his time at these organizations, Mr. Roche joined Heidrick & Struggles in 1964, where he became Senior Vice President and Eastern Manager in 1973. Four years later he became Executive Vice President, responsible for all domestic operations.

A year later Mr. Roche became President and CEO. In 1981 he moved into the Chairman's role, permitting him more time to conduct high-level international search work. Thirteen years later Mr. Roche co-founded with John Thompson Heidrick & Struggles' Office of the Chairman.

Over his forty years at the firm Mr Roche has conducted CEO searches for companies including 3M; IBM; Gap, Inc.; PricewaterhouseCoopers; and Chubb Corporation.

About the Contributors

Mr. Roche is on the Board of the Community Anti-Drug Coalitions of America.

Richard T. Santulli is the former Chairman and CEO of NetJets, Inc., the company that has revolutionized private and corporate business jet travel through fractional aircraft ownership.

From 1969 to 1979, Mr. Santulli was an investment banker with Goldman, Sachs & Co., where he held various managerial positions, including Vice President of Investment Banking and President of Goldman Sachs Leasing Corporation. He earned his BA and MA degrees in applied mathematics and operations research from Brooklyn Polytechnic Institute.

In 1986, Mr. Santulli developed the successful NetJets program. In 1996, he introduced the NetJets Europe program, and in 1999 he inaugurated NetJets Middle East.

Mr. Santulli is a Director of the Andre Agassi Charitable Foundation.

Paul Skinner was named Chief Executive Officer of Shell Oil Products Company LLC in 2009.

Mr. Skinner spent forty years with the Royal Dutch/Shell group of companies, joining as a student in 1963. He served as the Chief Executive Officer of Shell's global oil products business from 1999 to 2003. He served as Managing Director of the Shell Transport and Trading Company PLC and served as its Group Managing

Director from 2000 to 2003. He served as President of Shell International Trading Company from 1991 to 1995 and was additionally responsible for the shipping business from 1995 to 1996. Mr. Skinner served as Director, Strategy and Business Services, Oil Products, from 1996 to 1998, and also President, Shell Europe Oil Products, from 1998 to 1999.

Mr. Skinner was formerly Chairman of Rio Tinto, the global mining and minerals company dual listed in the United Kingdom and Australia. He joined its Board as a nonexecutive Director in 2001, and became Chairman in 2003. He served as Chairman of the Board of Rio Tinto Plc and Rio Tinto Ltd. from November 1, 2003, to 2009, and also served as the Chairman of the Board of Rio Tinto Group from November 1, 2003, to 2009, when he became Chief Executive of Shell Oil Products Company.

Mr. Skinner has been Chairman of the International Chamber of Commerce (U.K.) since 2005. He has been a Director of Tetra Laval Group since 2005 and of L'air Liquide SA since May 10, 2006. He has been a nonexecutive member of the Defence Management Board of the U.K. Ministry of Defence since June 2006, and a member of the Board of INSEAD business school since 1999.

Mr. Skinner graduated in law from Cambridge University and has a Diploma in Business Administration from Manchester Business School.

About the Contributors

Barbara D. Stinnett is the President of Sum Total Systems, Inc., a market leader and a global provider of talent development solutions.

In 2003 Ms. Stinnett joined Sybase as worldwide Vice President and General Manager of the company's Business Intelligence Group. In 2004 she was promoted to the North American division and was responsible for the overall profit and loss of the organization, as well as for leading the direct and partner sales teams and building a customer-centric support organization for the region. Prior to joining Sybase, Ms. Stinnett held several positions at Hewlett-Packard, including Vice President and General Manager of Competitive Sales and Presales.

From 2005 to 2007, Ms. Stinnett served as Executive Vice President of Customer Operations and Chief Customer Officer of i2 Technologies, a supply chain organization committed to bringing low-cost supply chain solutions to their customers.

She then served as Head of Global Services and Senior Vice President of Services and Customer Operations at Silicon Graphics, Inc., which focuses on data management; developing, marketing, and selling computer servers; data storage; differentiation software; and visualization systems.

In July 2009 Ms. Stinnett joined SumTotal. In her current role, she is responsible for leading the company and its operations, with the mission of advancing SumTotal's integrated talent development strategy, while continuing to build best-in-class solutions around learning management, performance management, and compensation.

Rudy Vidal is the former Executive Vice President and Chief Customer Officer at inContact, Inc. (formerly UCN), which specializes in serving organizations with inbound call centers with ten to three hundred plus seats.

Currently Mr. Vidal is Principal of Vidal Consulting Group. In his role as consultant, he has helped *Fortune* 500 companies, emerging growth companies, nonprofits, and the education sector increase profitability and improve operational efficiencies through increased focus on the customer. His projects always provide hard, quantifiable ROI, and rely on policy, process, and delivery model leadership to drive results.

Prior to his development of Vidal Consulting Group and his work at inContact, Mr. Vidal was the Director of Extreme Customer Satisfaction at Panasonic and Panasonic Corporation of North America. His passion for customer centricity was awakened during his tenure at Panasonic Corporation of North America and by his study of the founder, Konosuke Matsushita. Mr. Vidal worked in the Matsushita family of companies for more than twenty-five years, becoming an integral part of setting strategy around customer satisfaction. His responsibilities included being a cultural change agent, dedicated to creating self-sustaining customer-driven cultures that encourage brand loyalty.

Mr. Vidal has served other *Fortune* 500 companies such as Samsung, Williams-Sonoma, eBay, and Bank of America, as well as small to mid-cap companies. He is the author of *Extreme Customer Satisfaction*.

Mr. Vidal graduated from New Jersey's Kean University in 2003 with a Bachelor of Science in Computer Science.

Dan Wittner is Chief Customer Officer at RBM Technologies, where he is responsible for global sales, marketing, business development, and client success. Founded in 2000, RBM Technologies provides complete in-store visual merchandising management solutions for large retailers. Among their clients are restaurants, fashion retailers, and banks.

Before joining RBM, Mr. Wittner was a managing partner at Satisfaction Services, Inc., which customizes mystery-shopper concepts for small and mid-tier retailers and manufacturers. Prior to this, he served as Vice President of Sales for PlumRiver LLC, which provides Web-based solutions for manufacturers and distributors of sporting goods and apparel.

Mr. Wittner was previously the Director of International Operations for Timberland Company, one of *Fortune*'s 100 Best Companies to Work For and 100 Best Corporate Citizens.

About the Contributors

Earlier in his career, Mr. Wittner held positions with Wilson Sporting Goods, a division of AMER, and with the Inter-American Development Bank. He holds a bachelor's degree in International Business from the University of New Hampshire and an MBA from Thunderbird, the American Graduate School of International Management.

⊰ ACKNOWLEDGMENTS ⊱

First and foremost, a heartfelt thanks goes to all of the executives who have candidly shared their hard-won experience and battle-tested insights for the *Lessons Learned* series.

Angelia Herrin at Harvard Business Publishing consistently offered unwavering support, good humor, and counsel from the inception of this ambitious project.

Kathleen Carr, Brian Surette, and David Goehring provided invaluable editorial direction, perspective, and encouragement, particularly for this second series. Many thanks to the entire HBP team of designers, copy editors, and marketing professionals who helped bring this series to life.

Much appreciation goes to Jennifer Lynn and Christopher Benoît for research and diligent attention to detail, and to Roberto de Vicq de Cumptich for his imaginative cover designs.

Finally, thanks to James MacKinnon and the entire 50 Lessons team for their time, effort, and steadfast support of this project.

THE LAST PAGE IS ONLY THE BEGINNING

Watch Free *Lessons Learned* Video Interviews and Get Additional Resources

You've just read first-hand accounts from the business world's top leaders, but the learning doesn't have to end there. 50 Lessons gives you access to:

Exclusive videos featuring the leaders profiled in this book

Practical advice for putting their insights into action

Challenging questions that extend your learning

FREE ONLINE AT:
www.50lessons.com/customers